W9-AYE-558

Lewis the Librarian

Written by Charnan Simon • Illustrated by Rebecca Thornburgh

Published in the United States of America by The Child's World®
PO Box 326 • Chanhassen, MN 55317-0326
800-599-READ • www.childsworld.com

Reading Adviser

Cecilia Minden-Cupp, PhD, Former Language and Literacy Program Director,
Harvard Graduate School of Education, Cambridge, Massachusetts

Acknowledgments

The Child's World®: Mary Berendes, Publishing Director

Editorial Directions, Inc.: E. Russell Primm, Editorial Director and Project Manager;
Katie Marsico, Associate Editor; Judith Shiffer, Assistant Editor; Caroline Wood, Editorial Assistant

The Design Lab: Kathleen Petelinsek, Design and Art Production

Library of Congress Cataloging-in-Publication Data

Simon, Charnan.
  Lewis the librarian / written by Charnan Simon ; illustrated by Rebecca Thornburgh.
    p. cm. — (Magic door to learning)
  ISBN 1-59296-624-1 (lib. bdg. : alk. paper)
  1. Librarians—Juvenile literature. 2. Libraries—Juvenile literature. I. Thornburgh, Rebecca
McKillip, ill. II. Title. III. Series.
  Z682.S57 2006
  020.92—dc22   2006001630

A book is a door, a magic door.
It can take you places
you have never been before.
Ready? Set?
Turn the page.
Open the door.
Now it is time to explore.

Lewis the librarian loved his job.

5

He loved opening the
door in the morning and
turning on the lights and
smelling all the books.
But that wasn't his
favorite thing.

Lewis loved looking
in catalogs and
ordering new books.
But that wasn't his
favorite thing.

He loved mending
old books and putting
them back on the
shelves. But that wasn't
his favorite thing.

Lewis loved sorting magazines and
newspapers and CDs and DVDs.

But that wasn't his favorite thing.

13

Lewis especially loved
helping people find just
the perfect book to read.

14

But that wasn't his favorite thing.

Lewis didn't mind if people
talked in his library, as long
as they weren't too loud.
Lewis liked hearing people
help each other and teach
one another new things. But
that wasn't his favorite thing.

Lewis loved working at the check-out counter and handing out stamps and stickers.

But even that wasn't his favorite thing.

What Lewis *really* loved was collecting a stack of books with great stories and great pictures, pulling up a chair, and reading aloud to children who visited the library.

And THAT was
his favorite thing!

23

Our story is over, but there is still much to explore beyond the magic door!

Did you know that you and your friends can create your own library? Each of you should pick five favorites from all the books you own at home. Tape a notecard on the inside of each book. Try to get together with your friends once a week to exchange different books. Every time you lend out a book, remove the notecard and write your friend's name and the date you let her borrow it. This will help you keep track of where your books are. Be sure to share what you thought of each book when you and your friends get together!

These books will help you explore at the library and at home:

Prieto, Anita, and Renee Graef (illustrator). *B Is for Bookworm: A Library Alphabet.* Chelsea, Mich.: Sleeping Bear Press, 2005.

Thompson, Carol, Paula Craig, and Bobbie Houser (illustrator). *Mr. Wiggle's Library.* Columbus, Ohio: Waterbird Books, 2003.

About the Author

Charnan Simon lives in Madison, Wisconsin, where she can usually be found sitting at her desk and writing books, unless she is sitting at her desk and looking out the window. Charnan has one husband, two daughters, and two very helpful cats.

About the Illustrator

Rebecca Thornburgh lives in a pleasantly spooky old house in Philadelphia. If she's not at her drawing table, she's reading—or she's singing with her band called *Reckless Amateurs*. Rebecca has a husband, two daughters, and two silly, unhelpful dogs.